I0794745

discovermore

Exploring Primary Sources

Exploring the Emancipation Proclamation

Sarah Schmidtt

Britannica Educational Publishing

IN ASSOCIATION WITH

THE ROSEN PUBLISHING GROUP

Published in 2025 by Britannica Educational Publishing (a trademark of Encyclopædia Britannica, Inc.) in association with The Rosen Publishing Group, Inc.
2544 Clinton Street, Buffalo, NY 14224

Distributed exclusively by Rosen Publishing.
To see additional Britannica Educational Publishing titles, go to rosenpublishing.com.

Editor: Brianna Propis
Cover Design: Michael Flynn
Interior Design: Rachel Rising

Photo Credits: Cover (series background) Dai Yim/Shutterstock.com; Cover, Science History Images/Alamy Stock Photo; p. 5 https://commons.wikimedia.org/wiki/File:Civil_Rights_March_on_Washington,_D.C._(Leaders_marching_from_the_Washington_Monument_to_the_Lincoln_Memorial)_-_NARA_-_542010.jpg; p. 5 Wendy van Overstreet/Shutterstock.com; p. 6 Morphart Creation/Shutterstock.com; p. 7 https://en.m.wikipedia.org/wiki/File:Emancipation_Proclamation_WDL2714.jpg; pp. 7, 11, 17 kilic inan/Shutterstock.com; p. 8 https://commons.wikimedia.org/wiki/File:Black_cotton_farming_family.jpg; p.10 https://commons.wikimedia.org/wiki/File:Harriet_Tubman_1895.jpg; p. 11 $150 Reward. $150 reward cut of runaway slave Ranaway from the subscriber, on the night of the 2d instant, a negro man, who calls himself Henry May, ... William Burke, Bardstown, Ky., September 3d. Bardstown, 1838. Pdf. Retrieved from the Library of Congress, <www.loc.gov/item/2021767324/>.; p. 12 https://en.wikipedia.org/wiki/File:Frederick_Douglass_(circa_1879).jpg; p. 13 https://commons.wikimedia.org/wiki/File:Battle_flag_of_the_Confederate_States_of_America_(3-5).svg; p. 14 https://commons.wikimedia.org/wiki/File:1846-47_John_Brown_by_Augustus_Washington_%28without_frame%29.jpg; p. 15 https://commons.wikimedia.org/wiki/File:Border_Ruffians_Invading_Kansas_by_F._O._C._Darley.jpg; p. 9 The Miriam and Ira D. Wallach Division of Art, Prints and Photographs: Photography Collection, The New York Public Library. "Slave Quarters, South Carolina." The New York Public Library Digital Collections. 1860 - 1920. https://digitalcollections.nypl.org/items/510d47d9-aa84-a3d9-e040-e00a18064a99; p. 16 crbechervaise/Shutterstock.com; p. 17 https://commons.wikimedia.org/wiki/File:Recruiting_poster_New_York_Mounted_Rifles.jpg; p. 18 Bacon & Co. Map of the United States, showing the territory in possession of the Federal Union, January. [London Lithographed by Bacon & Co, 1864] Map. Retrieved from the Library of Congress, <www.loc.gov/item/99447141/>.:; p. 19 https://commons.wikimedia.org/wiki/File:Winslow_Homer_(American,_1836-1910)_-_The_War_for_the_Union,_1862_-_A_Cavalry_Charge_-_1942.1258_-_Cleveland_Museum_of_Art.jpg; p. 20 COURTESY ABRAHAM LINCOLN FOUNDATION, UNION LEAGUE OF PHILADELPHIA; p. 21 https://en.m.wikipedia.org/wiki/File:Emancipation_proclamation.jpg; p. 22 luma_art/Shutterstock.com; p. 13 https://commons.wikimedia.org/wiki/File:Angelina_Emily_Grimke.jpg; p. 23 https://en.m.wikipedia.org/wiki/File:Scott-anaconda.jpg; pp. 25, 27 Everett Collection/Shutterstock.com; p. 25 https://commons.wikimedia.org/wiki/File:Col._Robert_Gould_Shaw_by_Horace_R._Burdick.jpg; p. 26 https://commons.wikimedia.org/wiki/File:Lincoln_assassination_slide_c1900_-_Restoration.jpg; p. 28 Crative Studio Design/Shutterstock.com; p. 29 scoutori/Shutterstock.com.

Library of Congress Cataloging-in-Publication Data

Names: Schmidtt, Sarah, author.
Title: Exploring the Emancipation Proclamation / Sarah Schmidtt.
Description: [Buffalo] : Britannica Educational Publishing, an imprint of Rosen Publishing, [2025] | Series: Discover more: exploring primary sources | Includes index.
Identifiers: LCCN 2024030847 | ISBN 9781641903783 (library binding) | ISBN 9781641903776 (paperback) | ISBN 9781641903790 (ebook)
Subjects: LCSH: United States. President (1861-1865 : Lincoln). Emancipation Proclamation--Juvenile literature. | Enslaved persons--Emancipation--United States--Juvenile literature. | United States--Politics and government--1861-1865--Juvenile literature. | Slavery--United States--Juvenile literature.
Classification: LCC E453 .S36 2025 | DDC 973.7/14--dc23
LC record available at https://lccn.loc.gov/2024030847

Manufactured in the United States of America

CPSIA Compliance Information: Batch #CWBRIT25. For further information contact Rosen Publishing at 1-800-237-9932.

Contents

Firsthand Account

If you were interested in learning about the past, how would you choose sources to examine? History students may study both primary and secondary sources. A primary source is a firsthand account made by somebody who lived during that time. News articles, photographs, documents, recordings, and memoirs are all examples of firsthand evidence of the past.

A secondary source is created after that time by someone who did not experience it for themselves. An example of a secondary source is a biography written about someone from the past whom the author didn't know personally. Secondary sources are usually written after gathering information from primary sources.

One person's interpretation, or feelings based on their experiences, of an event may be very different from another person's. Primary sources reflect these individual points of view and allow students and historians to draw their own conclusions.

The 1963 March on Washington for Jobs and Freedom was one of the most important protests in U.S. history. A photograph from this protest is a primary source.

compareandcontrast

How are primary and secondary sources alike? How are they different?

A biography written about Martin Luther King Jr. is a secondary source.

A Voice for the Voiceless

Primary sources are important when studying America's history of **slavery**. In the past, many societies had slavery. The trade of enslaved Africans across the Atlantic Ocean began in the early 1500s. European ship captains "bought" people who had been forced into slavery from African traders. The ship captains then brought the enslaved persons to the Americas, where Europeans had established colonies. Conditions on slave ships were terrible, and many people died. Those who survived were sold to people who forced them to work. The first enslaved Africans in what would become the United States arrived in the English colony of Virginia in 1619.

Ships' crews treated enslaved Africans like cargo and forced too many of them into small ships for transport. Between 1501 and 1867, enslavers kidnapped about thirteen million African people and forced them onto European and American ships. The enslavers then sent them across the Atlantic Ocean and forced them into slavery.

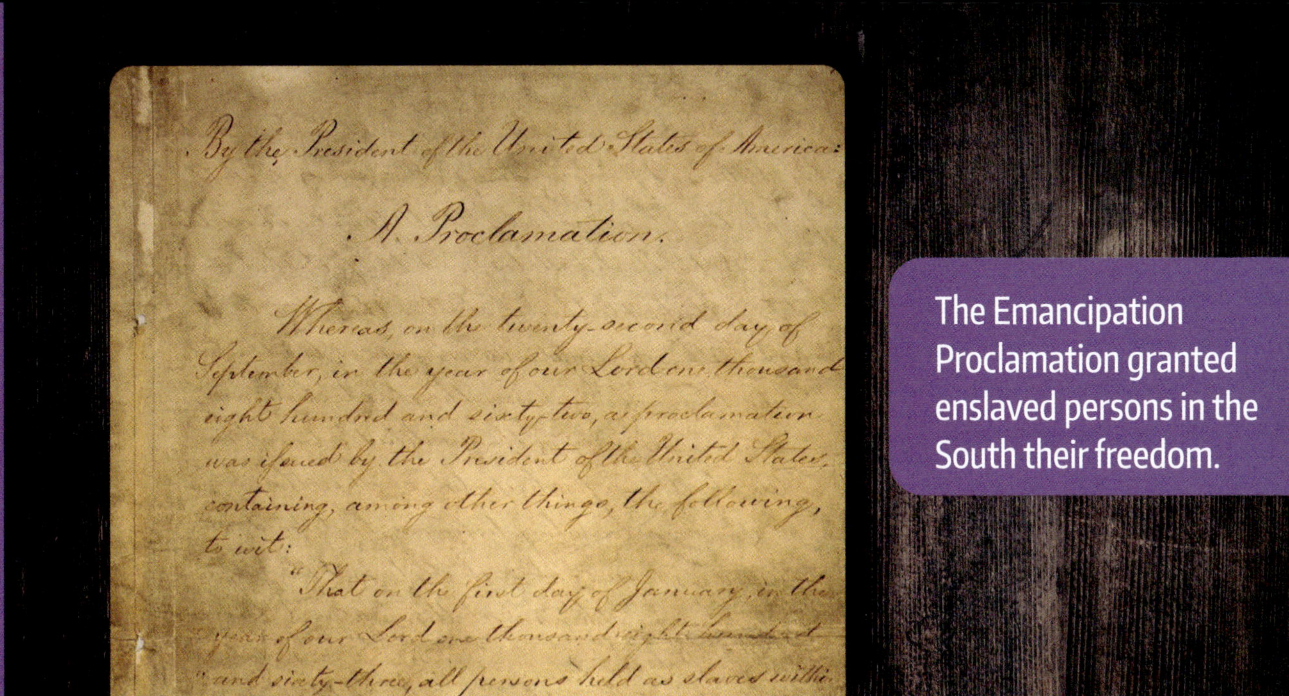
By the President of the United States of America:

A Proclamation.

Whereas, on the twenty-second day of September, in the year of our Lord one thousand eight hundred and sixty-two, a proclamation was issued by the President of the United States, containing, among other things, the following, to wit:

"That on the first day of January, in the year of our Lord one thousand eight hundred and sixty-three, all persons held as slaves withi

The Emancipation Proclamation granted enslaved persons in the South their freedom.

Accounts by people who were once enslaved are a primary source for studying slavery. It provides them with a voice during a time when they weren't able to have one. Ads looking for enslaved runaways are primary sources, too. Another primary source is the Emancipation Proclamation, a document issued during the American Civil War. It declared that the enslaved individuals in the southern states were free.

WORD WISE

SLAVERY IS THE INSTITUTION OF PEOPLE BELIEVING THEY "OWN" OTHER PEOPLE. ENSLAVED PERSONS WORK FOR THESE ENSLAVERS WITHOUT PAY AND MUST DO WHATEVER THEY FORCE THEM TO DO.

Slavery in the South

Before the American Revolution, the British government allowed slavery in all its thirteen North American colonies. However, most enslaved persons were on farms in the South. Southern plantation owners who grew tobacco and cotton forced enslaved Africans to work in their fields and harvest their crops. The northern economy came to rely mostly on manufacturing. Paid workers kept mills and factories running.

Overseers expected enslaved persons to pick 200 pounds (91 kg) of cotton per day. Some enslavers whipped those who picked less.

Plantation owners forced enslaved persons to live in small huts known as slave quarters. They often slept on straw on the floor of these one-room buildings.

In the 1700s, some people in Britain began to speak out against slavery. They started the abolitionist movement, an effort to end slavery. By the time of the American Revolution, an abolitionist movement had started in the British colonies, too. Beginning with Vermont in 1777, state governments banned slavery in each of the northern states.

Large plantations in the southern states still depended on slave labor. Even after the U.S. government halted the Atlantic slave trade in 1808, enslavers forced the children born to enslaved women into slavery themselves.

Consider This

Why do you think state governments in the South permitted slave labor for longer than state governments in the North?

Moral Disagreements

Enslaved persons suffered immensely. Many state governments banned them from learning to read or write. The law allowed white landowners to "buy" and "sell" the enslaved as if they were animals and even to split up families. The enslavers often gave harsh punishments to the enslaved. Some of the enslaved managed to escape to the North, traveling in secret. They were helped by people who formed a system called the Underground Railroad.

After escaping slavery herself, Harriet Tubman helped many enslaved persons flee to the North.

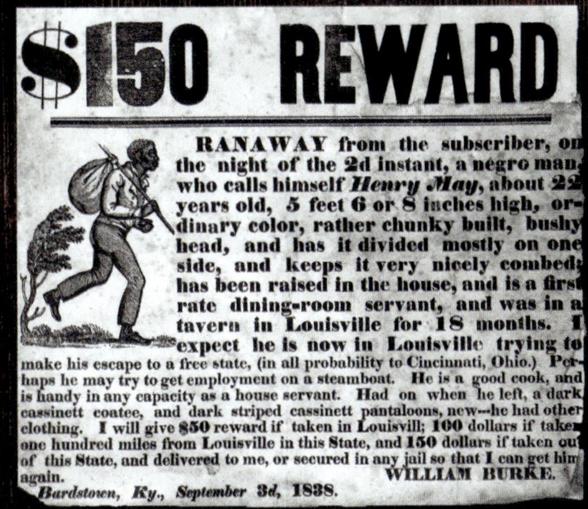

$150 REWARD

RANAWAY from the subscriber, on the night of the 2d instant, a negro man, who calls himself *Henry May*, about 22 years old, 5 feet 6 or 8 inches high, ordinary color, rather chunky built, bushy head, and has it divided mostly on one side, and keeps it very nicely combed; has been raised in the house, and is a first rate dining-room servant, and was in a tavern in Louisville for 18 months. I expect he is now in Louisville trying to make his escape to a free state, (in all probability to Cincinnati, Ohio.) Perhaps he may try to get employment on a steamboat. He is a good cook, and is handy in any capacity as a house servant. Had on when he left, a dark cassinett coatee, and dark striped cassinett pantaloons, new--he had other clothing. I will give $50 reward if taken in Louisvill; 100 dollars if taken one hundred miles from Louisville in this State, and 150 dollars if taken out of this State, and delivered to me, or secured in any jail so that I can get him again.

WILLIAM BURKE.

Bardstown, Ky., September 3d, 1838.

When an enslaved person ran away, enslavers posted ads offering large rewards for the return of their "property."

In 1793 and 1850, the U.S. Congress passed laws called the Fugitive Slave Acts. These laws required that if Americans captured the enslaved people who escaped, they had to return them to the enslavers in the South. The laws applied even if an enslaved person was captured in a state where slavery was outlawed. White Americans could also kidnap free Black people and force them into slavery.

The Fugitive Slave Acts angered a lot of abolitionists in the North. Tensions began to rise between northerners who morally disagreed with slavery and southerners who didn't, eventually leading to violence.

Consider This

Those who escaped knew they would face harsh punishment if they were caught. Why do you think they still chose to run away?

Fighting Back

Abolitionists protested the Fugitive Slave Acts by helping the enslaved to escape. The abolitionists risked going to jail if they were caught breaking the law. They also spoke out against slavery in books, speeches, and more. Some religious leaders criticized slavery in their sermons.

In an 1838 speech, southern-born abolitionist Angelina Grimké Weld talked about slavery. She said, "I know it has horrors that can never be described. . . . I witnessed for many years its demoralizing influences and its destructiveness to human happiness."

Frederick Douglass learned how to read and write in secret because the law banned enslaved persons from learning such things.

In 1836, Angelina Grimké Weld published her pamphlet *An Appeal to Christian Women of the South* to urge southern women to join the antislavery movement.

Frederick Douglass, who was formerly enslaved, also made powerful arguments against slavery in speeches and books. In his memoir, *The Narrative of the Life of Frederick Douglass,* he described his view on songs sung by the enslaved: "They breathed the prayer and complaint of souls boiling over with the bitterest **anguish**. Every tone was a testimony [demonstration] against slavery and a prayer to God for deliverance from chains."

WORD WISE

ANGUISH REFERS TO BEING IN A STATE OF EXTREME DISTRESS AND PAIN, MENTALLY OR PHYSICALLY.

Proslavery and Antislavery

As the United States gained more land to the west, Americans had different opinions about whether the new territories should allow slavery. Northerners wanted to stop the spread of slavery. The abolitionists formed a political group called the Republican Party.

People in the South believed in "states' rights." They wanted each state to decide for itself whether to allow slavery. Most of the southern economy depended on cotton and tobacco, and those crops were picked by the enslaved.

In 1856, an abolitionist by the name of John Brown and his sons killed five proslavery advocates in an act of violence known as the Pottawatomie Massacre.

Many proslavery people from Missouri crossed the state line to vote on election days in Kansas to try and turn the outcome in their favor. They became known as border ruffians.

One of the new U.S. territories was Kansas. There, proslavery and antislavery supporters fought and killed each other over the issue of slavery. This time of violence was called "Bleeding Kansas." Eventually, the abolitionists won. In 1861, Kansas joined the United States as a free state. But the violence pushed Americans even closer to a civil war.

Consider This

Today, it is legal for a person to vote only in one state—even if they are registered to vote in more than one. Why do you think this is?

Sparking a War

Abraham Lincoln was a member of the Republican Party, which opposed slavery. When Americans elected Lincoln president in 1860, white southerners were angry. Southern states decided to **secede** from the United States and form their own government. The people of the Confederate States of America, or the Confederacy, elected Jefferson Davis as their president.

Eventually, eleven states joined the Confederacy. The northern states that remained loyal to the United States were called the Union. Some slave states on the border between the North and South did not secede. They remained a part of the Union. Many Americans still hoped to avoid going to war.

Today, Abraham Lincoln's legacy is rooted in him paving the way for civil and social freedoms for Black Americans.

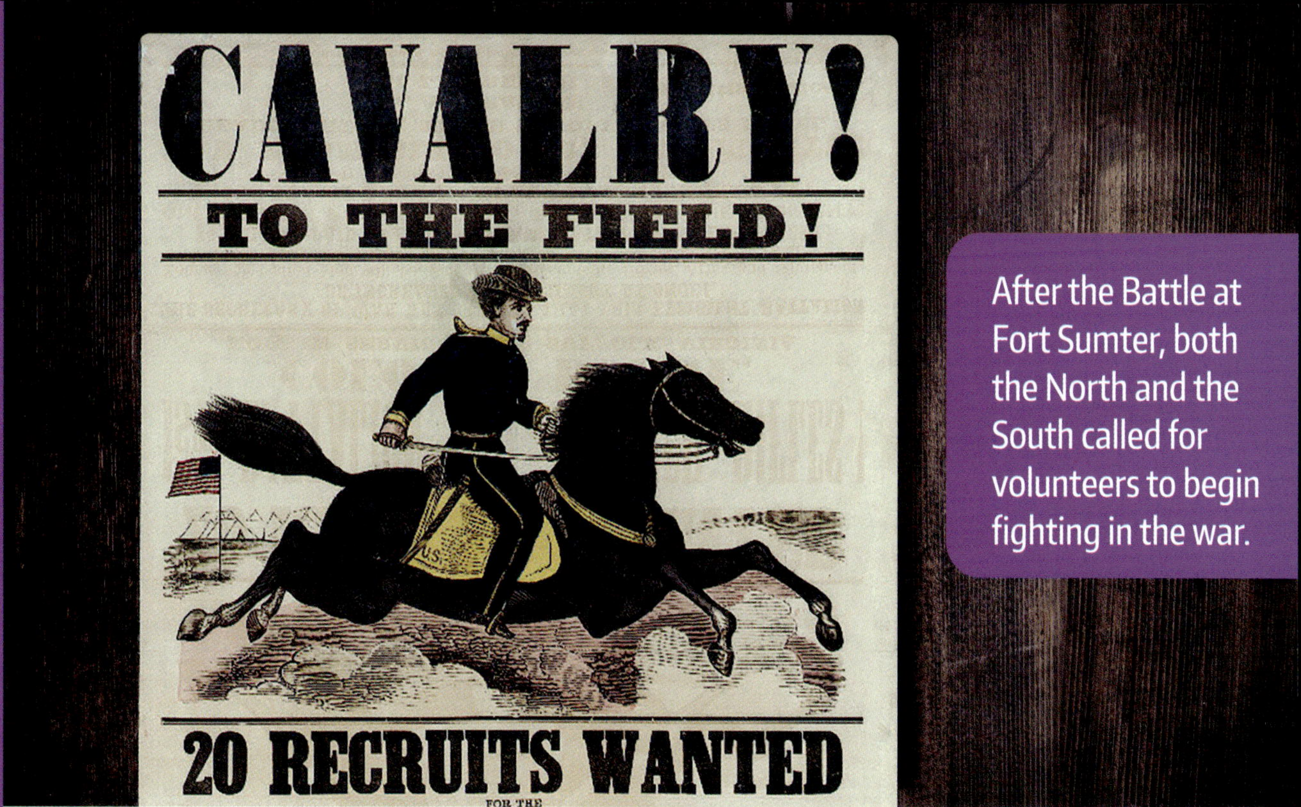

After the Battle at Fort Sumter, both the North and the South called for volunteers to begin fighting in the war.

On April 12, 1861, Confederate troops attacked U.S. government forces at Fort Sumter in Charleston, South Carolina. The Confederates overpowered the fort and the U.S. forces surrendered. The attack on Fort Sumter sparked the beginning of the American Civil War. Fighting between Union and Confederate forces lasted from 1861 until 1865. Hundreds of thousands of people died during the war.

WORD WISE

TO SECEDE REFERS TO FORMALLY WITHDRAWING FROM, OR LEAVING, A GROUP OR ORGANIZATION.

First Draft

When the Civil War began, abolitionists wanted President Lincoln to emancipate, or free, every enslaved person. Lincoln refused. He believed that his main purpose was to save the Union and to keep the states united. He worried that if he freed the enslaved, border states such as Kentucky and Delaware might join the Confederacy.

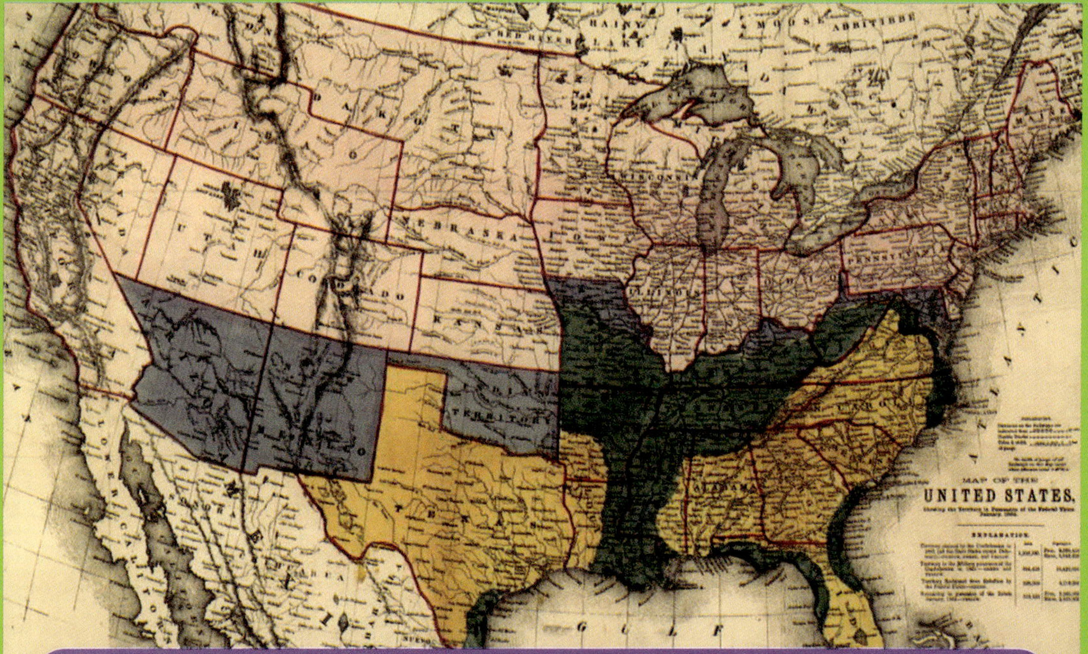

This map shows where the important battles of the Civil War took place. Most of the battles were fought in the southern states.

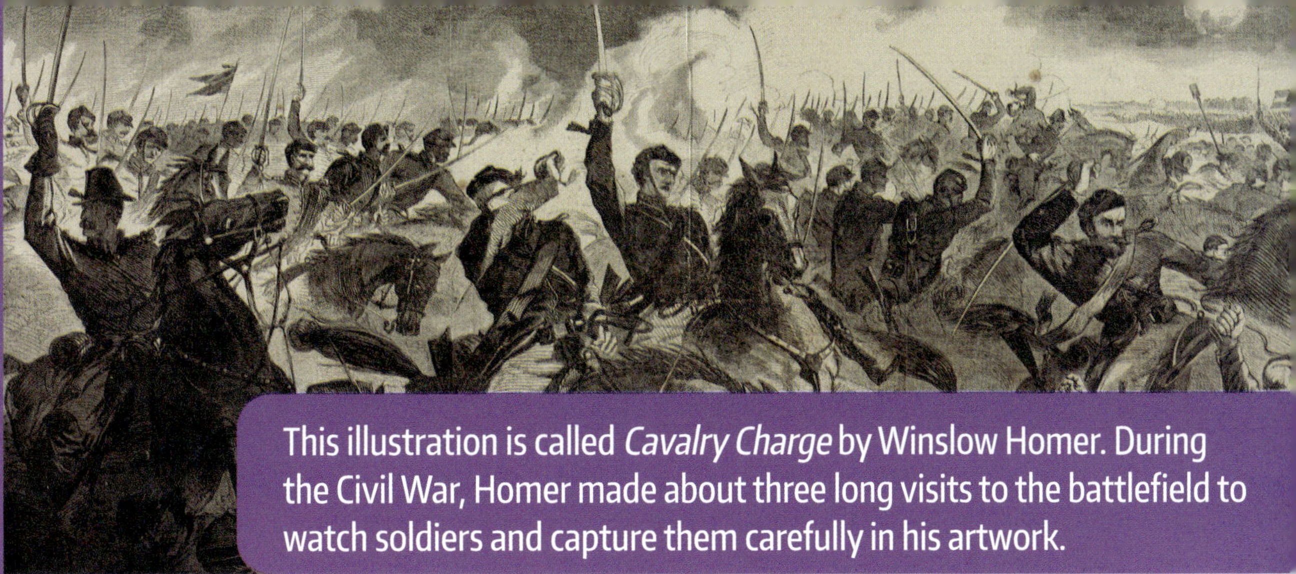

This illustration is called *Cavalry Charge* by Winslow Homer. During the Civil War, Homer made about three long visits to the battlefield to watch soldiers and capture them carefully in his artwork.

Lincoln wrote a draft of the Emancipation Proclamation in July 1862. The war was less than a year old, and the Union armies had suffered serious defeats. Secretary of State William Seward worried that freeing the enslaved might make people believe the Union couldn't win without help from the enslaved. Seward convinced Lincoln to wait until a big Union victory.

After a string of losses, Union forces managed to hold back the Confederate army at the Battle of Antietam on September 17, 1862. This was Lincoln's chance. Five days later, he released a **preliminary** version of the Emancipation Proclamation.

WORD WISE

A PRELIMINARY VERSION IS AN EARLY VERSION OR DRAFT OF SOMETHING.

A Fight for Humanity

The preliminary draft of the Emancipation Proclamation stated that as of January 1, 1863, "all persons held as slaves within any state . . . in rebellion against the United States, shall be then . . . forever free." If the Confederate states did not stop their rebellion, then the proclamation would go into effect on January 1, 1863. On that day, those enslaved living in states at war with the Union would be free.

This portrait of Abraham Lincoln was made to honor his role in the fight for emancipation. Under his arm is the Emancipation Proclamation.

President Lincoln wrote the Emancipation Proclamation on a single piece of paper, double-sided.

On January 1, 1863, President Lincoln issued the final version of the Emancipation Proclamation. The proclamation didn't actually end all slavery in the United States. It didn't apply to the border states, which were not in rebellion against the Union, and it was ignored by the Confederate states. However, the document changed the meaning of the war. The fight to save the Union became a fight for humanity and equality.

Consider This

After they were freed, some enslaved persons chose to stay on the plantations where white landowners previously forced them to work. Why do you think they did this?

Different Ideas

The Union's intention to end slavery was made apparent with the Emancipation Proclamation. And that would make all the difference. President Lincoln commanded the U.S. military to guard the freedom of the formerly enslaved: "The executive government of the United States, including the [army and navy] . . . will recognize and maintain the freedom of [emancipated] persons." The Confederacy, on the other hand, was fighting to preserve slavery, a practice that most civilized nations now considered **immoral**.

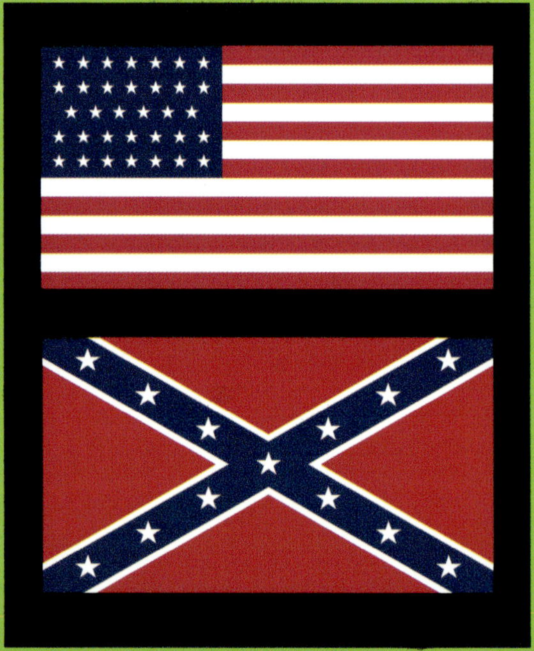

Both the Union and Confederacy thought the war would be over after a few months. When it was clear it would last longer, they had to find new ways to fund their causes.

Union ships blocked the Confederacy from exporting cotton for money to pay for the war. This plan was nicknamed "Scott's Great Snake."

Near the beginning of the war, the South believed that European countries, such as Britain and France, would support them. The southern landowners thought those countries needed the cotton from their plantations. Some countries did consider supporting the Confederacy. But after the Emancipation Proclamation was issued, most foreign support lay with the North.

WORD WISE

IMMORAL MEANS EVIL AND WRONGFUL.

Inequality in Combat

The Emancipation Proclamation declared all enslaved persons in the Confederate states free. It also declared "that such persons of suitable condition will be received into the armed service of the United States." That meant that the emancipated enslaved could serve in the Union army.

As soon as Union soldiers captured a region, they gave the enslaved their freedom. Almost 180,000 of those freed joined the Union army. Another 19,000 served in the navy.

The Emancipation Proclamation said the Union would fight to end slavery. The emancipated enslaved believed passionately in the cause they were fighting for. The new Black recruits gave the North a real advantage in the war. They impressed their white commanders with their bravery in battle. However, Black soldiers faced unequal conditions throughout the war.

Robert Gould Shaw was a Union officer in the Civil War who was proud to lead his Black troops in battle. Other officers showed resistance toward the Black troops.

compareandcontrast

Think about how Black soldiers were treated during the Civil War. Both Black and white Union soldiers were held captive as prisoners throughout the war. How do you think the Confederates treated Black soldiers compared to white soldiers?

One of the injustices Black soldiers faced while fighting in the Civil War was unequal pay. The U.S. Army paid Black soldiers $10 a month, while white soldiers received $3 more. Black soldiers also had the cost of their clothing taken out of their pay, unlike white soldiers.

Continued Fight for Freedom

On April 9, 1865, the Confederacy surrendered to the Union. Six days later, Abraham Lincoln was killed. Later that year, the Thirteenth **Amendment** to the Constitution ended slavery in the United States. Additional amendments made Black Americans U.S. citizens and gave Black men the right to vote.

Abraham Lincoln was assassinated, or killed, by a man named John Wilkes Booth, who wanted to renew the Confederate cause by eliminating the leader of the federal government.

The Fifteenth Amendment granted Black men the right to vote in 1870, but Black women did not receive the same right until many years later.

Before the war, the southern economy and culture depended on slavery. Even after the U.S. government freed the enslaved, life was still difficult for most Black Americans. Many whites did not see Black people as their equals. White southerners used violence to stop Black people from voting and to keep them from making a new life for themselves.

The South was destroyed by the war and had to be rebuilt. During the Reconstruction period between 1865 and 1877, the North and South worked to put the United States back together. They often disagreed about exactly how to do that.

WORD WISE

AN AMENDMENT IS A CHANGE OR ADDITION TO A PRE-EXISTING LAW.

A Fair Society

After the war, an organization called the Freedmen's Bureau set out to help newly freed Black individuals. Millions of people were in search of food, medical care, and education. But Reconstruction did not provide land for the free Black men and women. As of a result, many of them became sharecroppers, which was part of a farming system that kept Black Americans in poverty. New laws—called Black codes—limited their activities and freedoms. The laws made sure southern whites stayed in power.

Juneteenth is a federal holiday celebrated on June 19 each year to mark the end of slavery in the United States.

In the United States, February is Black History Month.

The Emancipation Proclamation is housed in the National Archives in Washington, D.C., and is set to be on permanent display in 2026. It is one of the most important documents in U.S. history. Yet more than 160 years later, racial inequalities still exist in the United States. The Emancipation Proclamation was the first step toward creating a fair society where every individual can share the same rights, privileges, and opportunities.

Consider This

Why do you think the government put laws in place to keep Black individuals from having some freedoms after the Emancipation Proclamation? Why do you think this was allowed?

Glossary

archive A collection of historical documents and records.
cavalry A group of soldiers who fought on horses.
document A written or printed paper giving information about or proof of something.
draft A rough copy of a written document.
economy The way a country runs its industry, trade, and finance.
firsthand Something obtained through someone's personal experience or observation.
fugitive Someone who is running away, especially from the law.
legacy Something handed down from one person to another.
memoir A story of a personal experience.
pamphlet A small booklet.
plantation A large farm that is worked by laborers.
privilege A special right or advantage given to a person or a group.
recruit A newly enlisted member of the armed forces.

For More Information

Books

Jones-Radgowski, Jehan. *The Emancipation Proclamation Inkstand.* North Mankato, MN: Capstone Press, 2022.

Miller, J. P. *Juneteenth.* Minneapolis, MN: Jump!, Inc., 2024.

Meadows, James. *Slavery.* Mankato, MN: The Child's World, 2021.

Websites

Britannica Kids: Abraham Lincoln
kids.britannica.com/kids/article/Abraham-Lincoln/345491
Read more about the president responsible for the Emancipation Proclamation: Abraham Lincoln.

Civil War Battles Interactive Map
mrnussbaum.com/civil-war-battles-interactive-map
By clicking on a location on this map, you can learn about the important events during the Civil War that happened there.

National Geographic Kids: Black History Month
*kids.nationalgeographic.com/history/article/black-history-*month
Learn more about the significance of Black History Month.

Publisher's note to educators and parents: Our editors have carefully reviewed these websites to ensure that they are suitable for students. Many websites change frequently, however, and we cannot guarantee that a site's future contents will continue to meet our high standards of quality and educational value. Be advised that students should be closely supervised whenever they access the internet.

Index